HANDS OF THE MAYA

VILLAGERS AT WORK AND PLAY

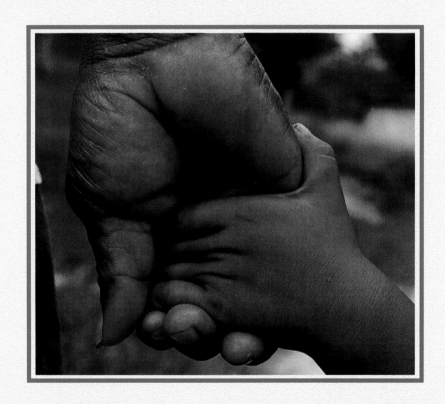

RACHEL CRANDELL

HENRY HOLT AND COMPANY · NEW YORK

Henry Holt and Company, LLC, *Publishers since 1866*
115 West 18th Street, New York, New York 10011

Henry Holt is a registered trademark of Henry Holt and Company, LLC

Distributed in Canada by H. B. Fenn and Company Ltd.

Library of Congress Cataloging-in-Publication Data
Crandell, Rachel.
Hands of the Maya: villagers at work and play / Rachel Crandell
1. Mayas—Belize—Juvenile literature. 2. Mayas—Industries—Juvenile literature.
[1. Mayas. 2. Indians of Central America—Belize.] I. Title.
F1445.C73 2002   972.83'004974152—dc21   2001002076

ISBN 0-8050-6687-X
First Edition—2002 / Designed by David Caplan
Printed in the United States of America on acid-free paper. ∞
1 3 5 7 9 10 8 6 4 2

If you'd like to contact the Maya Centre Community, please write to:
Liberato Saqui, P.O. Box 141, Dangriga, Belize, Central America

Dedicated to the Maya parents

whose loving, creative, persevering hands

are both teacher and example

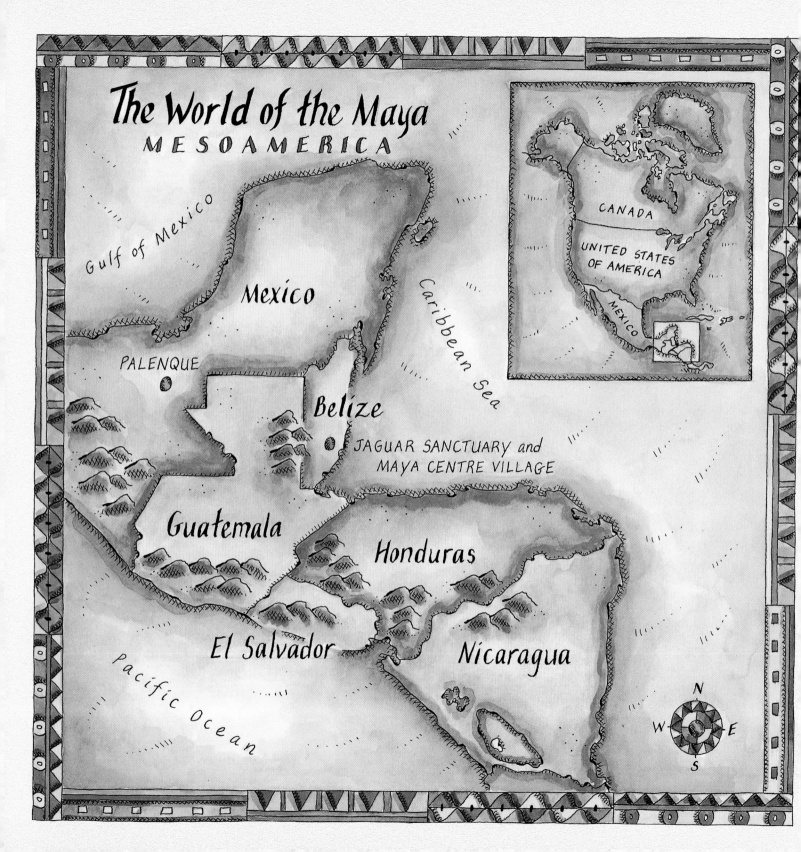

Maya hands are seldom still. Most of the daily work of Maya Indians is done by hand, the way their parents and grandparents have taught them. They live and work close to the earth. Their hands feed, clothe, shelter, nurture, and celebrate.

Since about 320 C.E. Maya people have lived in what we know as Mesoamerica, in southern Mexico and the countries of Belize, Guatemala, Honduras, and El Salvador. Today the Maya speak one of more than twenty variations of the Mayan language and follow many of the same customs as their ancestors.

I am an elementary school teacher, and my students are pen pals with Maya children in Belize; we share our cultures through letters and drawings. English is the official language of Belize, because until 1982 it was a British colony called British Honduras. The children in Maya Centre speak Mopan Mayan at home and English at school, but many Mayas also speak some Spanish and even Creole, if they live near the coast. On my visits to Maya villages in Belize and Guatemala I take photographs to show my class when I return. On my last trip I stayed for many months. I lived in Maya Centre Village, Belize, at the edge of the Jaguar Sanctuary. I slept in a hammock in a palm frond house they built for me. I bathed in the river, listened to Maya stories, and ate wild pig, barracuda, and paca with my friends. They showed me how to dig cassava with my machete, carry firewood with a tumpline, and scrub my laundry on a flat rock in the creek. I learned to catch fish in a trap, dig slate out of the riverbank, and make tortillas very round. I tried my hand at carving in stone, stalking jaguar in the night, paddling upriver in a canoe, and sleeping in the forest where we found tapir tracks.

The Mayas taught me a lot about cooperating and taking pride in work well done. They know the wisdom of "many hands make light work." Some jobs are too big to do alone and more fun to do together, like building a house. Satisfaction comes from successfully planting corn on a steep slope, skillfully weaving rich natural colors into a traditional design, or making a house completely from trees, vines, and leaves of the forest.

I went to live with the Maya and to learn from them. I returned home with a great admiration for their way of life. In a world where so many things happen by pushing a button, I celebrate skilled hands at work.

Every day in a Maya village there is work to do.
Nicolasa is up early. Her tender hands keep her baby
son warm and safe.

Maria helps her brothers bring firewood from the forest before she goes to school. A *tumpline* over her head makes it easier to carry the heavy load. Maria's mother needs a lot of firewood for cooking three meals a day.

Breakfast always includes *tortillas* toasted on the *comal*.
But today Dora and Yollie prepare an extra large chicken
caldo and a mountain of tortillas for lunch because . . .

. . . this is a special house-building day. Everyone helps. Grandfather passes the *cohune* palm leaves to the men on the roof, where they tie them in place with vines. The leaves will keep the house dry for six years.

Since it's the end of the dry season, it is a good time to sow *maize*. Eladio is planting maize in last year's *milpa* with his only tool, a *xu'ul*. After harvest, the kernels are removed by hand before being ground into *masa* for tortillas.

Each morning, Dominica and the other women take the family's laundry to the creek. Dominica gives the *hammock* a thorough scrub on the flat washing stone.

While her older brothers and sisters are at school, Iliana puts her hands to work caring for the family's animals. Even young children play an important role in daily life. Wool from the sheep will be spun into yarn for her mother's weaving.

Maya hands are never idle. On their *backstrap looms* the mothers are weaving cloth to make *huipils*. You can tell which village a family is from because the women weave the same traditional designs their great-grandmothers taught them. Each pattern is distinct to its own village.

Grandmother Apolonia has gone to market for the day to weave and sell her baskets.

After school, Sarita takes time to practice carving in *slate*. Her mother teaches her to carve a design from an ancient Maya temple at *Palenque*. Sarita's father brings the stone from the riverbank in the forest and scrapes it smooth with his *machete*. They can sell the carvings at the Women's Co-op. They help one another by taking turns working at the shop when tourists come to buy.

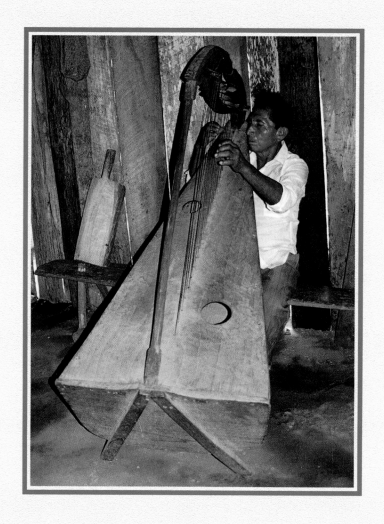

Tonight begins a special seven-day celebration of music and dance. Eusebio built his own *aj ché arpa* from trees in the forest. His haunting music sounds like the melodies plucked from the strings of ancient Maya harps.

Elogorio plays his *marimba* with three sticks. The balls on the sticks are crafted from *latex,* and the chambers below the keys are made of different-sized *calabashes.* Imagine four men playing the marimba at once. You couldn't help dancing at the celebration!

At the end of a long day in a Maya village, it's comforting to be held by your grandmother or grandfather. Strong, gentle hands feel just right.

GLOSSARY

AJ CHÉ ARPA (ahj chay AR pa): A wooden harp.

BACKSTRAP LOOM: A simple loom that may be suspended from a tree, hook, or house post and strapped around the back of the weaver.

CALABASH (KA lah bash): A hollow gourd used as a container, an instrument, or a utensil.

CALDO (KAHL doh): A hot soup often cooked with spices.

COHUNE (kah HOON): A palm tree whose large leaves are used for making house roofs, its nuts used for cooking oil, and the tender top eaten as heart of palm.

COMAL (koh MAL): A large, flat cooking surface, which was made from clay in ancient times but is now made from metal, like a griddle.

HAMMOCK: A hanging bed of woven netting, suspended by cords at each end.

HUIPIL (whee PEEL): A Maya woman's blouse.

LATEX (LAY tex): Sap of a rubber tree.

MACHETE (mah CHE tay): A long-bladed knife used as a tool for cutting, digging, slicing, and chopping.

MAIZE (mayz): Corn.

MARIMBA (mah RIM bah): A musical instrument native to Central America, made from forest trees; resonators below the keys are made from wood or gourds; the wooden keys are struck with rubber-balled sticks to create a lovely sound.

MASA (MAH sah): Wet, softened ground corn used as dough.

MILPA (MEEL pah): A garden or field for crops.

PALENQUE (pah LEN kay): An ancient Maya city in southern Mexico famous for its temples, pyramids, and the tomb of Pacal (a ruler in the seventh century C.E.).

SLATE: A black rock that can be broken into slabs and is easy to carve.

TORTILLA (tor TEE yah): A round, thin, flat, unleavened bread made of corn or wheat flour and cooked on a comal, hot stone, or griddle.

TUMPLINE: A strap over the head attached to a load carried on the back; useful for transporting firewood, vegetables, or even a baby.

XU'UL (shool): A digging stick the ancient Maya used for planting that is still used in remote villages today.

DATE DUE

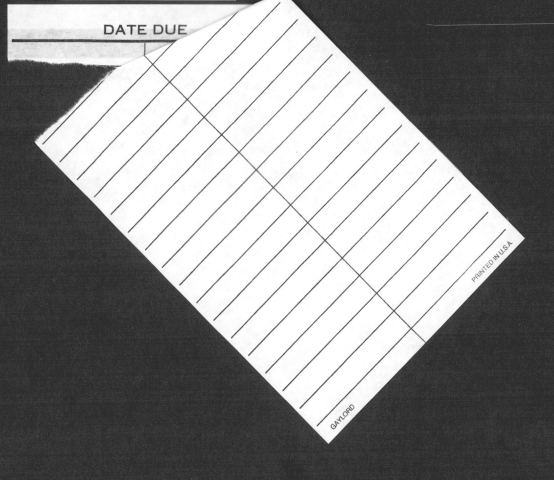

GAYLORD

PRINTED IN U.S.A.